ABOUT THE AUTHOR

David Mason has worked as an immunopathologist, a sales training manager and has owned a restaurant. He began writing in 1993; his first book was produced in 1996. He works in schools teaching children to write stories and poems. He has six wonderful children and a lovely wife. They live in Norfolk in a happy, noisy house.

"Teacher's Cauldron" © David J. Mason 2004

Publishing address:
North Street Publishing, 1 North Street, North Walsham, Norfolk NR28 9DH
Telephone: 01692 406877
Web: www.InspireToWrite.co.uk
Email: DavidMasonPoet@AOL.com

Illustrations © Nick Walmsley 2004
Contact address: Tryddyn, Horning Road West, Hoveton, Norfolk NR12 8QJ
Telephone: 01603 782758

British Library Cataloguing-in-Publication Data
A catalogue record for this book is available from the British Library
David J. Mason
ISBN: 0 9521326 4 8

All rights reserved. No part of this book may be reproduced or utilised in any form or by any means, electronic or mechanical, including photocopying, recording, or by any information storage and retrieval system without permission in writing from the Publisher.

By the same author:

"Inside Out"	Poetry 1996
"Speaking Out"	Audio collection 1997
"Get a Life"	Poetry 1997; illustrations by Nick Walmsley
"Seven Summers"	Poetry 1998
"Leo's Magic Shoes"	Children's novel 1999; illustrations by Kirsty Munro.

Reprinted in 2000 as "Pedro's Magic Shoes" with illustrations by Nick Walmsley

"The Great Sweetshop Robbery"	Children's poetry 2001
"Handy Andy has the Candy"	Children's poetry 2001
"Go Teddy Go"	Children's CD poetry-songs 2002
"The Elf who sang the King to sleep"	Children's fables and fairy tales 2002
"Living in another world"	Children's poetry 2003
"After Midnight"	Children's novel 2003

Produced by
Skippers Print & Design
53a The Green, Martham, Great Yarmouth, Norfolk NR29 4PF
Telephone: 01493 740998

Table of Contents

Lipstick 5
Poo at the pool 6
When I am away 8
Special friend 9
Quiet, please 10
A Year Six teacher from Penzance 11
Fooling God 12
Ghost train 14
Raining flowers 16
Fidgety 18
Henry's eyes 19
Teacher's cauldron 20
Class rules 22
The wonder of woodlice 24
My special friend 25
Sad Sam 26
Cracked 28
Tell-tale 30
The wasp 32
Grandma 36
First day 37
God is rock and love 38
Severyone's 41
Prolific policemen can't stop scoring 42
Blowing raspberries 43
Carry 44
Outside 45
Spilling drinks 46
Killer skimmer 48
Mrs. Kimby's Gobweed 50
Death to the alarm clock 52
London lives 53
If only flowers could talk 54
Epitaph for the famous 56

Table of Contents continued

Tooth fairy 58
On the other foot 60
Family feast 62
Premiership poetry 65
From the top to the bottom 66
Lion 68
On a wet afternoon 69
Dragon 70
Johnny Wharton 73
He won't hurt you 74
Fishes 76
Boyz n'the bak 78
Hope 80
Rory goes the wrong way 81
Brothers and sisters 82
Clapham Junction 85
Isn't life funny? 86
Waterloo 87
Go to da clinic (e-motion) 88
Bedtime blues 90
Pedetrians, where are you? 92
Don't run me over 94

Lipstick

Luscious and full
But too much lippy
Just a bit, see
Moist and slippy
Lose my grippy
What a pity
I know they're pretty.
But far too tricky
Wet and drippy.
Too much spitty
Bit more gritty
Nice and nippy
In a jiffy
Wipe the lippy
Honey – kiss me!

Poo at the pool

A sudden change I did discern
Appeared upon young Lily's face
A sudden switch from serene smile
A thoughtful look, a true grimace.
Alarm bells ring inside my head
I stand up to attention
A grin on our young Lily's face
Tells tales too rude to mention.
No time to waste, I whisk her out
She sits upon the pool side.
Think quick, think quick, I tell myself
Nowhere to run, nowhere to hide.
To the shower! I command
We move with some aplomb
Together we can save the world
From Lily's hidden bomb.

Now guys, let me explain to you,
She is the youngest daughter,
Some things you can do in pools
And some things you ought no to.
"Daddy, she has done a poo!"
I beg them, "Not so loud",
Lily standing smiling there,
Of the poo she is so proud.
Repeating deep inside my head,
"Ladies – cool, gents – stay calm,
Nobody wants to hurt anybody
Nobody wants to come to harm."

I'm searching, then I catch it
I have it in my hand
The brown grenade I rush to save
And flush it down the pan.
"You have to clear the area,"
I hear the lifeguards say,
There's more where that one came from
That deadly brown grenade.

Back at the explosive scene
I'm cleaning up again
Pushing all the shrapnel pieces
Down the shower drain.
And so the bomb disposal squad
Has saved the day once more
We salute you swimming public
We keep clean your pool.
And Lily, you're diffused now
It's time to bathe again
We can swim in safety
Down at the shallow end.

When I am away (for all my children)

Your form misshapen, uncertain size
Floats across my scaled eyes
Playing tricks upon my mind
You in misty corners hide
And I try oh yes I try
To snatch a glimpse of smile
But stolen by another child
Out of reach a thousand miles.

A gnawing emptiness inside
Heavy weight this wasted time
Suspended till a turning tide
Brings me groaning back to life
Stealing close to see you sleep
I realise my distant dream
To touch the real, bone and skin
Feel myself a whole again.

Special friend

This special friend
I held his hand
And he in turn
Took mine
A special place
In this cold world
He was thoughtful
He was kind.
He took away my loneliness
He taught me many things
He took away my emptiness
And brought me still more friends
And more till I at once forgot
What sadness was about
No longer tears and mumbled fears
I want to sing, I want to shout!
And tell the whole world not to worry
One day they'll have a friend
Who's warm and caring, smiling face
On whom you can depend.
This special friend
I shook his hand
And tears ran down my face
This special friend
Let go my hand
Left for another place.
This special friend
Left me his hand
I hold it, day to day.
This special friend
Left me the love
That will not go to waste.

Quiet, please

Right! All of you! You've done it this time!
Driven me to it! I want silence, silence,
Silence, silence, silence, silence, SILENCE!
Thirty hearts sounded hollow
Thirty pairs of ears heard the echo.
Thirty sets of eyes glazed
As dull cardboard statues.
No movement, none at all, not a limb.
If dropped you might hear it
But still, no sound from falling pin.
In this classroom life has frozen.
Dare you move the clock on?
Dare you take one peek at him?
His form unblinking, staring,
A brow unfurrowed, uncaring.
Restful, thoughtful, perfect peace
His shape suggests to the outside world
And reluctantly to us.
I cannot believe in him
Polished form of sandpaper smooth
Voice which gravel, would crackle
And grate, but in this second of truth
Whispers on the wind
Like ether to us,
Silence, thank you class.

A Year Six teacher from Penzance

A teacher who came from Penzance
Once threatened to pull down his pants
He said look at me
But the kids wouldn't see
So deep was their tortuous trance.

The same man we mentioned before
Said, hey kids I'll give you what for
He was fire and flame
But the kids stared the same
And said they were terminally bored.

Fooling God

All dead animals live in the sky
Above where planes to Majorca fly.
Can we, can we go to that place?
Meet with God in his heavenly base?
Because up there is where God stays,
Flying you catch a glimpse of his face.
But here on earth the animals are alive
And they won't see God until they die
And it's the same for children, mums and dads,
Aunties, uncles, grandpas and nans.
But I'm going to trick God
I have a plan:
Tonight after tea instead of our bed
We'll lie down in the grass and pretend to be dead.
Daddy –
You won't be scared and you won't be cold
Snuggle up to me and we'll be brave and bold.
I'll hold your hand when you're frightened of the dark
And save you from wolves who live in our park.
Don't worry Daddy do just like me
Stay very, very still just like this – see.
Then we'll wait and very soon
God will come down from his home near the moon.
He'll be sad and sorry for us
Coming close, he'll give you a kiss.
He'll think that we are dead and gone
But coming close we'll prove him wrong.
Fooled you God, we're not dead!
Me and Dad we joked instead

And God he'll smile and
Get the joke
And disappear in a
Puff of smoke.
I'll never forget that look on his face
And all those dead animals floating in space.

Ghost train

Off goes the ghost train
A slow and steamy start
Bright silver wheels gleaming
In the winter's evening dark.
Black curtains at the window
Dare you take a peep?
The carriages are empty
Or so... it...would... seem.
They're picking up a little speed
Billowing clouds of smoke
I watch from the embankment
Is someone shovelling coal?
Strange shadow in the red light
Hunched back of fireman
Who feeds the hungry engine
And the ghost train rattles on.
Rattles on and on and on
And faster faster still
I see the ghost train rushing by
From the old abandoned bridge.
Sparks they are a-shooting
In the clear cold frosty night
The whistle sounds a toot-toot-toot
As the ghost train flashes by
And on to the next station
Crunch and scrape of brake
Jolting of the carriages
Shuddering and a shake.
And then an eerie silence

I wait and wait and wait
At last the click of carriage door
I try to run – too late!
Out come the ghosts
I hide behind the mist
They make their way through station
Across the lonely street.
Up the hill they trudge
In one long ghostly line
Their heavy bodies double bent
With the passing of their time.
They turn into the churchyard
Past the creaking gate
Each one to a gravestone
Each one stops and waits.
Then all at once they fall
And sink into the ground
Into their watching grave
And never to be found.

Come and ride the ghost train
Special midnight trip
Visit all your favourite haunts
Before you rest in peace.

Raining flowers

Grey geranium clouds appear
Tinged with deeper red
We feared the rain was coming
But flowers fell instead!
A mist of droplet daisies
Signalled break of day
Then a heavy shower of snowdrops
Tumbled from the sky.
The flowers fall persistent
Their stem and sepals heavy
Torrential multicolour
The petal flutter steady.
Puddle pelargoniums
Lay upon our street
Flower proof-ed wellies
Protect our pansy feet.
Streams of bright narcissus
Down our gutters roll
Heavy scents are blocking drains
The system cannot cope.
Rivers of red roses
Through the valleys roam
Sweeping all before them
Onward to the coast,
Where swimming in the sea
Splendid the surfinia
And the whales and the dolphins
Are bathing in the nectar.
In the distance lightning striking

Close by the thunder boom
Mushroom clouds of poppy seeds
Make dark the day but soon...
...Bluebell sky is filling
Intense the heavenly glow
Brilliant the sun appears
A daffodil yellow.

Fidgety

Fidgety bottom
Can't sit on one:
No, no not at all
Fidget in classroom
Fidget in hall –
What's in his pants?
Spiders and ants!
What's in his brain?
A runaway train!
And what's in that bottom?
A nervous hip-hoppin!
A fidgety rhythm
A bottom a-jifflin'.

What is the problem?
It's me and my bottom!
I tell it to stop
But it just keeps on shufflin'
It's a fidgety bottom
No-one can stop him.
What will he do?
Disturb me and you.
What shall we do?
Take out the strong glue.
Stick to the floor
Fidget no more!

Henry's eyes

Henry's eyes they love the sun
Beams down on his chocolate skin.
In dancing rays those eyes do glow
Little Henry's summer show.
While spacemen look for another planet
And a little bit of life there in it
They ought to explore young Henry's eyes
Glittering galaxy glowing surprise.

Teacher's cauldron

Eye of toad and leg of frog
Spines of prickly hedgehog.
Insides of slug, his sticky slime
The black bits of maggots all crawling in line.
Heads of spiders crunchy and black
Wriggling worm front and back.
Greenfly, blackfly, cockroach shell
Rotting eggs and their foul smell.
A pinch of brain, a little ear
A toenail there, a toenail here.
Bluebottle tongue, jellyfish jelly
Fatty bits of fatty belly.
Mealy grub and crocodile
Dogfish, catfish, squirming eel.
Piggy's trotter, kidney, liver
Slippery fish skins shining silver.
Nose of dog and cheek of cat
Wing of crow and tail of bat.
One hundred crawling caterpillars
A thousand snails with gooey innards
All steamed in breath from stagnant pond
Mixed up with my magic wand.
Black and thick, oh deadly drink
Tell me children what you think.
So my pretties take a look
Attention please, put down your books
Your pencils and your paper too
Scissors, paint and sticky glue.
Now look straight into teacher's eye

Repeat these words beginning with "I
Will always pay attention
Do as my teacher asks
I'll go about things quietly
Never chatter in class.
I'll never fidget, never fuss
Courteous, so polite
Never pull of scratch or punch
And never pick a fight.
Always patient loving child
Never mean and snappy
The most important think each day
To make my teacher happy."
Or else my pretties
I'll take a cup
And make you drink
The whole lot up!
Delicious drink from teacher's cauldron
Special brew for naughty children.

Class rules

We must always be polite and put our hands
Up and not call out
And not scream
And not shout
And not jump up and down, or feign a fit
Or run out
Of our school, even when we'd like to.
We must not accept lifts from Martians
Who promise to take us away from all of this
Nor ask the Martians if they
Would take away Miss.
We must not giggle or wriggle or juggle
Grumble or mumble
Or wish that we were always playing football.
We must work hard at all times
And not gaze out of the window
Dreaming of a promised land
Of adventure, fun, sea and sand.
We must not look to the birds of the sky
And wish that we, like them, could fly
Away from all of this.
We must listen when others are speaking.
We must not fiddle with our pencils, hair,
Nose, teeth, ears, paper, chair
Or next-door neighbour.
We must listen attentively
And look as if we care
About what they have to say
Even though we'd love to be far away.

And we must remember too
Our teacher would like to break the teaching rules
But this is her classroom
And the Government tells her what to do.
We must not be glad when
Our school is closed because it's snowed
Or because it is found to be structurally unsafe
Or under threat from a passing mudslide or
A local volcano.
No, we must wear a contented smile
Upon our face
And show that during school times we love
To be in this place.
We must not plot incendiary
Or experiment with nuclear devices of any kind.
No we must always bear in mind
This, my friends, is our school
Forget the Martians and the Government
My friends – our classroom rules.

The wonder of woodlice

Why not buy a woodlouse?
This shy and charming pet
Sometimes as still as statue
You'd think that he was dead
But then at once he comes to life
And scuttles on his way
And waves a friendly leg or two
And bids you "Sir, good day".
But do be careful handling
Place neatly on the palm
Do not drop or squash your catch
Don't cause your woodlouse harm.
Place your lice inside a bag
Take them anywhere
Do not show to adults
You might give them a scare.
Remember, please your woodlouse
He likes to dine on plants
Loves the darkest places
Especially people's pants.
Now the woodlouse he is loving
He is patient kind and true
He doesn't cost so much to feed
He'll eat your rubbish too.
So next time when considering
A cheap and faithful pet,
Choose the woodlouse
They're so cute-the best pet you can get.

My special friend

I don't want to be
Given over to the care of other people
Dressed as a doll in some shop window
Told not to talk by the boom of your TV
Left in my room to amuse myself on screen.

I don't care for this comfortable home
All those belongings that leave me cold.
Don't want a club or society
I just want you to come with me.
Take my hand on this childish journey
Come in close, share some secrecy.
Oh yes I am a child, greedy
But only for the time you give me.

Forget the passing passions, fashions
The friends I make, so many –
The one friend I have always wanted
I'll grow up and you won't know me.

Sad Sam

Sad Sam stood
His head hung down
In the foggy black
Of the school playground.
He tried to laugh
He tried to smile
But his face it
Would not move a muscle.
He wanted to say
Things weren't that bad
He'd said it before
But this time was sad.
The other kids laughed
And the other kids smiled
But Sam simply stood
With a blank in his mind.
His eyes they glazed over
His feelings were dead
For if Sam came alive
He would cry out instead
And ask them why
They called him names
And wouldn't let him
Play their games
And couldn't for
One second see
That Sam had
Feelings, yes indeed.
Well once he did

But now no more
I've locked me in
And shut the door
And school and
All this fear and dread
I won't let it
In my head.
And Sam he
Trudges into class
Hoping school
Will quickly pass
And Sam at home
Lay on his bed
Dreaming of a
World instead.

Cracked

I don't know who invented it
Some say a stupid game
But stand outside the gates at three
The tension's mounting just the same.
But we don't think it's stupid
It's a thinking person's game
It's cunning and planning and careful procedure
It's bold as brass and not scared of pain.
It's excitement, danger, dicing with death
We may never survive to tell
And all those kids who said we were stupid
They'll wish they wished us well.
Yes they'll miss us in the classroom
Stare at the empty seat
Their eyes awash with salty tears
They'll cry themselves to sleep.
They'll miss us in the football team
They'll miss us when we're gone
Without their captain, centre half
The team can't carry on.
But there's no time to wonder
Fearless we must step forth
And pray for skill and good luck
We might survive the course
That stretches long and lonesome
A mile down the road
Where mines lay hidden under cracks
One step they will explode.
One false step you've had it

There is no looking back
There's fire and flames and choking smoke
When you step on the crack
And when the cracks come closer
That's when the going gets rough
That's when you must hold your nerve
And tell yourself you're tough.
I'm tough and I can make it
My home just round the corner
But will I see my folks again
My mother, father, brother?
I panic, I'm not looking
Foot falls upon the crack
"Goodbye folks!" I yell out
There is no going back
To the life that was before this
Somehow I crawl on home
To tell my Mum I'm dead
One step I did explode.

At first she didn't answer
Then Mum looked straight at me
Before you go to Heaven son
What would you like for tea?

Tell-tale

The tell-tale sits
In her tell-tale cage
Singing the sad song
Of shock and outrage.
Oh miss I can hardly
Bring myself to say
And tell of all the bad things
That happened on this day.
Though weak is my voice
And sad is my heart
I surely must endeavour
To tell you from the start.
With tears in my eyes
I will tell you the tale
Lest Miss I should
In my sad duty fail.

Well there's him who pulled her hair
And she who spat at him
And him who nicked your rubber
And 'er who took your pen
That one started shovin'
The other gave a kick
And this one said he's ill Miss
Well he's not really sick.
She it was who stuck the gum
And that kid moved the seat
The clumsy kid who's grinning now
He tripped her with his feet.

The sly one ripped the picture
She drew on his book
That one there who wasted time
And wouldn't do his work.
He was passing notes round
It said "do you love me?"
And she was red and giggling
And wrote "I do" tee-hee.
There's the one who threw the rubber
And the other who dropped the pen
Not just once Miss, on the floor,
But over and over again.
He was copying her a bit
Then she was copying him
Then it started all of them
They was all of them copying.
That kid started talking
When you said "Be quiet do"
And the other ones were muttering
And laughing back at you.

So tell-tale sits
With her tell-tale smirk
Singing songs of sadness
Upon her tell-tale perch
But take care little tell-tale
As you do sit and scoff
One day they will find you out
And come and knock you off.

The wasp

Hot afternoon, sunny June
When wasp flies straight
Into our classroom.
Teacher says be sensible
Do not move
Quiet as a mouse
Still as stone
He's only a wasp
Let's all be calm.
But Samantha who is the silliest girl
In our class (and probably the whole world)
Giggling, fidgeting, making a fuss
Disturbed herself starts the rest of us.
"Samantha, sit down on your bottom at once!"
But Samantha is running from our friend the wasp.
Samantha starts Sadie who fluffs up her hair
And shrieks at the wasp she thinks is in there.
Says that her pigtails will fall out of place
And she will no longer be a princess
"Sadie stop fussing, my fragile child
I'm sure that your delicate frame won't be spoiled."

Then looney Billy gets in on the act
Likes to kill everything, totally mad
Starts swishing and swiping the air around him
His hard eyes a-gleaming, his monstrous grin.
Nervous Nick who sits next to Billy
Can't help himself and starts acting silly
He's read too many books on war
Says wasp is a bomber who'll give him what for.

"Watch out," he screams his guns are loaded
Wasp he dive-bombed and Nicky exploded.
"It's not funny you all heard the drone,
He's about to drop the big one don't leave me all alone."
Now hear the tale-tellers to add to the woe
Millions of stories of waspee gung ho!
Of kids who were stung in the mouth and the eyes
Bites that poisoned, maimed and paralysed
Big bites that swell to the football size
Stung kids in hospital, stung kids who died.
Now nervous Nick is jumpier than ever
Looney Billy has wasp-killing fever
Samantha she hides in the corner of the room
And Sadie she shrieks "I'm not coming to school!
It's a frightening place and no-one cares
Look at the tears and the state of my hair."
"It's alright for you, see I'm going to die,"
And Nick points to the wasp which is dive-bombing by.

Then it's the turn of the toady class helpers
The good-goodies who'll save the class from the chaos.
Don't worry Nick, Billy, Samantha and Sadie
We're the class helpers and we've come to save ye.
We'll finish the wasp, here come the swatters
They're cutting the air with their rolled up jotters
And now the class rises and joins in as one
The beginning of the end of our class has begun.
Everyone running and shouting and waving
Bumping and smashing and crying and wailing
And moaning and groaning with tears in their eyes
And shoving and pushing to win the wasp prize.

Then all of a sudden Miss screams, "That's enough!"
But it's not and the class carry on with their stuff
Deaf to Miss' screams and the voices of reason
And mad for a wasp in the wasp-hunting season.
So Miss tries again and stands on the chair
And jumps up and down to tell us she's there.
She's red-faced, she's crying, hysterical too
She's barking out orders, here's what you should do,
"Go back to your places, sit down, do not move!
Everyone silent – do not breathe a word.
Do not breathe a word or I'll squash you as well!"
Serious we see, by her red face we tell.
"OK class, there's just one last chance,"
Up on the sill Miss is starting to dance.
She moves toward window open wide too
Then bends down a little, she's going on through!
She's flapping her arms and pretending to fly
We're stunned into silence, will Miss have a try?
And leap to the shiny black tarmac below
Break every one of her beautiful bones?
Then Nervous Nick shouts, "No, Miss don't do it!"
And Mad Billy – well he's really lost it!
Doing the wasp dance and buzzing about
But Sadie can't see what the fuss is about.
Just look at me, I'm a terrible mess
Samantha has hidden her head in her desk.
"I will I'll do it!" shouts Miss from her perch
"You've driven me to it you miserable bunch."
And one of her legs is out of the window
The other is following surely but slowly.
Time ticks by in a dreadful slow motion
Even Mad Billy has ceased his commotion.

And none – not one – can really believe this
How one tiny insect could end it for Miss
And now we're all praying but Miss does not bluff
Miss on the ledge she's about to jump off.

Seconds left to save her life
When up jumps a toady just in good time
And shows Miss the head of the foulsome wasp
The rest of the body all broken and crushed.
Miss looks at the present, then blank-eyed stares
And a hush descends and no-one dares
Hope that Miss might change her mind
And slowly and surely she starts to climb.
On this hot afternoon, sunny June
Miss crawls back
Into our classroom.
Class says be sensible
Do not move
Quiet as a mouse
Still as a stone.
She's only a teacher
Let's all be calm.

Grandma

A kiss on paper thin skin
Be careful not to crush the ribs
A fragile heart beats
On thin pin limbs.
Grandma is shaking with excitement
A little unsteady but smiling
Warm to the touch
Grandma's not ready for dying.
I sit upon her knee
I listen to a story
Grandma tells of another world
Of a tiny excitable pig-tailed girl
Whose hands made a tree house.
She lived like a wild animal in a wood
And made a river den and hid
And played with the boys and was never scared.
I sit and gaze and wonder
Her shake won't last forever
She can use my Mum's skin cream
And we'll cook her up a big meal.
So now I feel much better
I'm not going to ask her
I know she'll live forever,
She must, my Grandma, I love her.

First day

Her eyes are brimming with tears
She struggles with a smile
To hide the deepest fears
She surely feels.
His hot hand clings to hers
His little boy's face says,
I don't know, I'm not certain,
Cross his heart, he draws a curtain.
He is a brave boy
A big boy does not cry
He checks for the smile in his mother's eye
His mother will not cry
One last good-bye.
He drags the cooling hand
Lifting makes a limp wave
In the harbour he sees her
Flag hands fluttering
I love you darling.
A wind of change blows him,
A turning tide takes him
Sailing into a classroom
All at sea, whilst she
Head bowed towards the empty buggy
Pushes on through crowds of mums
She runs, she runs, she runs.
Everyone else, so why not me?
But her heart moves the clock hands
Onward, onward relentlessly.

God is rock and love

Come on, said God
This is biggest
One you ever heard.
This is the greatest
Gig in the sky
It's me and the band
We're standin' by.
Now, just one more encore number
First let me introduce the band to yer.

On lead guitar, Saint Paul, formerly Saul
Got a real riff for you all
Hey, play Saul!
And on drums we have Saint Peter
The former Rock, now the Rock and Roller.
Solo Saint, bowl us over!
And on keyboards Saint John, your mystical man
Writes books full of meanin'
Music's full of rhythm.
Last not least, backing up the
Other boys in the band
Saint Mark, Saint Luke, bass, rhythm sound.
Finally so you get
The message real clear
It's me, God –
Can you hear?!
(-Yeah loud and clear
God, loud and clear.
Shouts the crowd through
This heavenly rock atmosphere.)

Yeah it's me on lead vocals
And tambourine
The angels, they're backin'
Sing like a dream.
Now, me and the band we want to say a big
Thanks to all you fans out there.
We know you've enjoyed the music so far,
Some of you seventy years of more.
But hey – we got one more song
And we know you're gonna sing along.
It's an old number one from the 1960s
But they're still playing this song on the radio nowadays
That band the Beatles they say they wrote it
Sad truth is the Beatles they stole it.
From God and his Band, inspired by me
It's called... (well angels sing sweetly)

He loves you yeah yeah yeah
He loves you yeah yeah yeah
Wait for it fellas, a 1-2-3-4

And with a love like mine
You know things can't be bad
Yeah with a love like mine
You know things can't be bad

I love you yeah yeah yeah
I love you yeah yeah yeah
I love you yeah yeah yeah yeah

And with a love like that
You know things can't be bad
Yeah with a love like that
You know things can't be bad

One more time
I love you yeah yeah yeah
I love you yeah yeah yeah
I love you yeah yeah yeah yeah

Thank you and good night.

And so, says God
My band did play
Some of the audience turned away
And it is the same today
Some won't listen to what I say
OK fellas, let's hear it again
I love you yeah yeah yeah
And with a love like mine
You know things can't be bad.

Severyone's

Smine, stiz
Snot, smine!
Stiz, smine
No way smine!
Maybe erz but snot yours
OK if snot mine, siz
Yeahhh sourz, not iz nor yours
Sure, OK, sourz, severyone's
Yeah OK severyone's stiz
Stiz, severyone's.

Prolific policemen can't stop scoring

Copper in a Vauxhall Viva
Says, "What you doing here?"
"We're only playing football."
"Well you'd better disappear."
Copper says we're trespassing
That this 'ere's for the school.
We tell him, he won't listen
We're here five days as a rule.
"But mister no-one's using it."
"That's not the point," he said,
"This 'ere land is Council land.
You can argue with them instead."
"Ah come on mister Copper,
Why don't you join in?"
"Oh alright then," said the copper,
"I'd like to be a kid again."
His uniform he took off,
We used it for the post,
And the copper got excited
When his team scored the most.
So when the siren rang out
He forgot to run and hide.
He's the first to be imprisoned
Whilst on the winning side.

Blowing raspberries

Raspberry yoghurt.
Raspberries with ice-cream,
Raspberry Pavlova
Or raspberries left alone?
Er, my favourite
The most yummy
The most funny
Is the raspberry
Blown on the body
Usually the tummy
And people passing by
Think that person's done
Something terribly naughty.

Carry

I do, it's true Daddy
I need a carry.
You love me you say
We sway
Under spell of chocolate
Eyes melting away –
Under the ray
Of brilliant kisses,
Your soft hand
Settles, squishes.
On my neck, five fingers tickling,
From the end to the beginning
Soothing every nerve ending.
I feel so wonderful
I see
That what the world cares is nothing
To me
As you cuddle
And snuggle
I struggle.
Aching, I climb
Your heart carried
So close to mine.

Outside

One step away from stifle
I open the door on
The Skipton night show
Whose list includes
A blushing red sky
A fallen September sun
Half a new moon
Hung over dew filled
Fields where silent sheep
Witness badger's secret snuffle
Mice run for cover
Skipton's night birds hover
Curtain black the show is
Over.

Spilling drinks

Good girl! She smiles and nods at me
You've drunk the whole lot up
Good girl! She waves a hand to me
To show the empty cup.
Bad girl! As I realise things
Aren't quite what I think
Close inspection shows the vessel
Floating in a sea of drink.
Never mind it's just the once
A harmless pool of water
Some would lose their patience
But I don't think I ought to
That is until I realise
There're other rivers flowing
Joining on the table top
A mighty ocean growing.
By now the calm has ebbed away
I feel myself a-frowning
The table cloth heaves one last breath
Before it dies of drowning.
What do you think you're doing?
But Dad it wasn't me!
Someone else's elbows
Her and him and she and he!
But the waters they are rising
No time to take the blame
We must take action now my friends
With six young lives to save.
Man the lifeboats, rubber rings

Set sail down the hall
To find the island they call lounge
Where there's no sea at all
Then I will do the mopping
Yes I will clear the mess
Clad in flippers, mask and pipe
And floaty safety vest.

So parents don't despair
At the loss of simple drink
As long as there's no drowning
It's not what you might think.
Let's face it drinking's no fun
It's so exciting to spill
To see your parents all at sea
Yes therein lies the thrill!

Killer skimmer

A boy in danger

A boy who holds the future

In an uncertain hand

He scours the land

Combing the sands

He has the plan

A boy, a decision

A moment, a mission

A boy like no other

Strange, a loner

He hides undercover

Until, one day, the waiting — is over

Juan-Carlos-Jesus-Iglesius-Sanchez is
Killer Skimmer

Hide if you will but there's only one winner
The Killer Skimmer

Co-starring
Anna-Maria-Rosita-Bonita-Real-Madrida

Skimmer's only friend

A beautiful girl

With a dark secret

And dyed blonde hair

She has the looks

He has no brains

A story of love, hate

And finally revenge...

Ah! Look out Mommy it's Killer Skimmer
Don't be so silly junior
Why he's only a kid
With a beautiful girl
Look out Mommy it's him
Don't be so silly calm down
Junior's right Ma'am
I am Killer Skimmer
But right now I have a stone in my hand
Right now I'm a dangerous man

Co-co-starring many other people
With unpronounceable Spanish names

Buena Vista Pictures present
Killer Skimmer
Life and death
There's only one winner.

Mrs. Kimby's Gobweed

Mrs. Kimby's Gobweed
The best you've ever seen
It'll snib your dibs if you diddle doodle
Cool your ming mong ming.

'Tis good for Kimby Lambas
For Kooly Mambas too
Show me the Gooly Ha Ha
Who's not afraid of you.

There's fing fong, will wong, nig nong
A little girl named Noom
All of them take Bogweed
Sleep sound on a snoob.

Then it's Mr. Sassoo
The Pooky Pally Noo
One spoonful of the Gobweed
He's a lovely bally hoo!

You've heard of Boolie Kanka
Whose scream will split your ears
Then give the Boolie Bogweed
No more Kanka tears!

Perhaps you have a Hoo Ha
At Hinky Honky's place
One sniff of the Gobweed
Nought but empty space.

Yes Mrs. Kimby's Gobweed
'Tis shocking but 'tis true
Let us remind the reader
Just what it can do:

Fing fong, will wong, nig nong
Ming mong, Lamba, Mamba
Paloo, Pooky, Noo Noo
Mr. Sassoo, Balla
A girl named Noom
One named Bool
A little Snoob
For a Ha Ha Gool.

Death to the alarm clock

Early morning leave me be
Softly in my sleepy sleep
Cosy where my breath makes deep
My mournful thoughts do flee this heap.
Alas alarm clock hear thee toil
So I ham-fisted smash and spoil
And crack that smile upon your face
Loose winged hands without a trace.
Now machine who lay in bits
Whose blood and guts were awkward spilt
Upon that coffin bedside table
From where you would my rest disable,
You buzzing one won't stir my soul
For free to Heaven flies your own
And I between soft silk can rest
The ticking heart beats in my chest.
Yes not until it strikes midday
When I have slept this morn away
I will confess, "Sir, I am late,"
And you, alarm will take the blame.

London lives

London lives, stretches her tentacles
London dips black toes in the Thames
And struggles to wake again.
London stumbles on roads
Littered with exhaust and noise
Her headache getting worse.
London seeks shelter
In the underground
Her heart flutters
With each passing bullet.
She can't stand it
And struggles to stalk streets
In open doorways under bridges they sleep
Cry out to touch London's long dark cloak
She passes by and dare not look.
London has an engagement
Makes a speech at Hyde Park Corner
Queues for cheap tickets
In London's little theatre.
London leaves the office
At seven-and-a-bit p.m.
Wonders at the millions of little Londoners,
Millions of them.
London can't sleep with the stress
And so calls up some friends –
Manchester, Liverpool, Birmingham and Leeds
Fancy a little get-together
Reach out and touch each other.
London loves to live it up,
Joke and laugh, dance and fun,
London leaves the lights on.

If only flowers could talk

My small eye saw light from the curtain
I knew then of something certain
I should go at once and visit them.
No creak, I crept down carpet stair
Soft on tip-toe to where
Magical key turns in magical lock – there!

They wait under dew drop shower
I know this morning, I sense their power
This magic garden, magical flowers.
But flowers will speak if you listen,
They clear their throats, their faces glisten
They bend your ear, you start to tune in.

"So hot I wish the Autumn would come
We're running out of water, each and everyone.
We're drooping under this August sun
We need water and we need food
Spare us a thought at your table do.
We produce such wondrous colours for you."

I told them not to worry, surely I'd take heed,
I'd bring them fresh water, fertiliser, feed
Bowing heads, they told me they were pleased.
One or two said "Please pick me."
Then tens, hundreds, thousands, high-pitched scream
The blooms did cry, cacophony.
"Quiet, quiet, quiet please."
My ears, this human, agony!

I'll bring a vase and fill it see!
And I do and the vase is overflowing
And a magic garden in my kitchen growing
And a miracle stands with no-one knowing.

Then tonight again I'll take the water
I'll hear the garden ring with laughter
Haunting songs from swaying stems sound
A gentle rhythm rolls from the ground
Tells of night and sleep to come
Darkness falls on the secret garden.

Then yawning, stretching, turn my eye
They whisper one more last good-bye
And my dreams are filled with magical powers
The sight and sound of magical flowers.

Epitaph for the famous

Fame is a fog
I can't find my way
Sunglasses by night
Sunglasses by day.
The signs point this way
And then to another
I'm tossed on the waves
And waiting for cover.
I arrive and they greet me
And show me the light
I wait in the darkness
Then learn to look bright.
I have a dress code
My world is a stage
I party all night
And I party all day.
I am extraordinary
I have achieved
All that you wanted
Is to be me.
Fill me with fame
Let it be real
I'm waiting too long
For the next meal.
Losing my grasp
My grip on the game
Empty vessel is
Lost without fame.

When I was famous
I hungered for more
Fallen from grace
I missed your applause.
The light is dimmed
Dead and gone
Fame is my label
The legend lives on.
Under the soil
We talk of our lives
The ones we enjoyed
The truths we denied.
So here on my tombstone
I asked them to write...

...I am so ordinary
Not much achieved
All that I wanted
Was to be me.

Tooth fairy

Tooth fairy, tooth fairy
Come to me
On your silk wings
Fly silently.
Across those streams and
Spreading willows
See what we've left you
Under our pillows.
Tooth fairy, tooth fairy
Come to me
Fly into my bedroom
Look! Can you see?
Reach underneath 'twixt my
Head and soft sheet
I've left it there for you
A wondrous treat.
Tooth fairy, tooth fairy
Come to me
How can you resist
The shining penny!
On what might you spend it
This glittering treasure
This money can bring you
Such infinite pleasure.
Tooth fairy, tooth fairy
Come to me
Look in my mouth
And do take pity.

See all the holes
Where once there shone white
See all the black ones
As dark as the night.
Tooth fairy, tooth fairy
Come to me
What do you give
For one silver penny.
One perfect tooth
To fill up the gap
One shining white
To exchange for a black.
Tooth fairy, tooth fairy
Come to me
They told me that you were
The one who gave teeth.
So tooth fairy, tooth fairy
How much for this gold?
A full set of dentures
Or so I've been told.

On the other foot

This morning my father
Would not get out of bed
I had to drag him downstairs
Make his breakfast myself.
Still he said
He wasn't hungry
And wouldn't look at me
And mumbled something unearthly.

I took him to his office
And was met by his nice boss
Who politely asked why it was
That my father didn't hand in his reports.
I looked at my father
His face said nothing
I left him standing to
Get on with my shopping.

After work my father
Insisted on two hours of TV
And when I asked, said nothing
Stared blankly at the screen.
"Good day at the office?"
Nothing came forth
And the TV talked to him
For what it was worth.

He took his tray of something and chips
And fiddled a bit with it

Before engaging with his pet computer
To email his buddies the whole world over.
"I have to go to parents' evening"
Clearly my father was not listening
And too busy with his mobile texting
To ever consider the medium of speaking.

"Your father is a very clever man
However he refuses to communicate.
You know how it is when people
Get to thirty something years of age.
Have you tried to talk to him?
Something on his mind?"
"I've tried and tried and tried," I say,
"He grunts but no more sound."

"Ah well I'm sure it all will pass
It's just a... a difficult time."
Yes, I'm sure and shake his
Hand and make my way back home
To find my father's bedroom a tip
And him sitting in the middle of it
Wearing headphones, blanked out vision
This picture of communication.

Family feast

You join us from the commentary position
One of the biggest meals of the season.
The dirty kits donned for this special occasion
There's shaking and banging – premature tension.
Players are warming – smashing of spoon
Shoving and pushing – I need more room!
And screaming and wailing and discordant song
Players are nervous they've waited too long.
But here it comes the game's begun,
Plate load of food they start with a scrum.
That's mind you've taken twice as much
You pig, you liar, you're such
A tell-tale you took more
I didn't, you did, so who's keeping score?
The adult refs are stuck in the kitchen
You join us back at the commentary position
Where food is flying all over the place
Most of it stuck to the hands and the face.
Some players are scoffing head down in the trough
Others refusing, no they've had enough
Some are so serious about their food
Others are messing, they're not in the mood.
In steps the ref – you'll have to eat that.
The player's refusing, he's answering back,
It's cold and it's pepper – I don't like the sauce!
Ref takes it away then – no pudding of course.
He's back at the pasta – he wants extra time
He wants to be there when the pudding arrives
He'll have to be careful – booked once this week

One more foul deed he'll be sent off his seat.
Meanwhile in the corner a scuffle breaks out
The ref's stepping over — what's all this about?
One of the players is throwing her dinner
Waving her hands, she says she's the winner.
Her plate is empty of that there's no doubt
But sucked and chewed contents lay scattered about.
The ref isn't happy — what's this all about?
And points to the player locating her mouth.
Back in the corner there's trouble ahead
The player's lost balance and is falling — instead
Of using four legs she's rocking on two
Claiming an infringement — the ref won't want to know
But barks at the player — get up on your feet
You haven't been injured, get on with your meal.
The older one is winning, experience does pay
Wolfing down the food in an attacking sort of way
But looking at his manners, he hasn't a defence
For pausing between mouthfuls does not make much sense.
The ref suggests he calms down and pauses for a while,
Try not to stuff your face full, she says with knowing smile.
The whistle blows, the game's up first half has been done.
The players they are arguing about the one who won.
The ref brings on the big cake, the second half begun
The players they get stuck in each and every one.
Just then a little miracle, the sound of silence rich
And peace and calm, tranquillity falls about the pitch.
The ref she leaves the stadium and settles for a drink
And joins us in the commentary box to tell us what she thinks.

Yes I would say on balance the older two won through
And when the pudding's finished we'll see what they can do -
They're going to the next round, they're made of sterner stuff
Join us at the commentary box to see them washing up.

Premiership poetry

Premiership poetry pays well,
Sponsorship writes my name on pens.
If I'm injured falling from the stage
And damage my poetic head
They'll bring on a substitute poet
To perform poetry in my stead.
I want to play poetry for England
In front of sixty thousand fans
At the Stretford Road End.
I want to compete in Europe
And play some Portuguese poetry.
I'd like to train at La Manga in Spain.
When I retire in my early thirties
With a gravelly voice and worn out verses
I shall teach some poetry
At the National poetry academy
Where poetic youngsters
Can learn about the game,
The heartache, the money,
The fortune, the fame.

From the top to the bottom

The crusher teeth came down
On frightened little Pip
"I surely am too young to die,"
So Pip he swam for it.
He launched into a whirlpool
Which sucked him down a pipe
He waved good-bye to daytime
And said hello to night.
Down the slide he sped
To big black bag below
The tummy churned and churned and churned
He floated to and fro.
Pip heard such terrible screams
He saw such awful sights
As other bits of lunch
Dissolved before his eyes.
The sandwich bits were softy
They didn't stand a chance,
You've got to have a tough skin
To survive the acid bath.
Through a trapdoor he did fly
To a helter-skelter ride
On and on through sausage links
Brave Pip – he might survive
The dungeon and the prison
The yawning tummy chasms
The di-gest-ion chemicals
The sausage tummy spasms.

Hours afloat in the soup he passed
To a special cubicle
And seconds later found himself
A-floating in the loo.
Down and down some more pipes
Then out into a drain
And onward to the sewage plant
Where they make the water clean.
They separated dear Pip
And in the mud he sank
And sat there waiting patiently
Upon the river bank.
The Spring sun came
And Pip he grew
In Summer
There were flowers too
And finally the deep red fruit
Hung upon his stem
And Pip – tomato plant stood proud
Above the rest of them.
From the top to the bottom
The throat to the tummy,
Brave Pip he made the journey
To make tomatoes – yummy!

Lion

The lion tamer cracked his whip
The lion did as the tamer said.
One day the tamer cracked too hard
The lion stops to search his heart.
The angry tamer cracked out loud
Lion of pride sat still and proud.
Whistling whip within an inch
Angry lion did not flinch.
Lion tamer whip on high
Roar, the lion split the sky.
Lion tamer will not stop
Lion gobbles tamer up.
Lion tamer he is dead
Lion spits out tamer's head.
Searches circus high and low
Finds a better job to do.
The lion he does crack his whip
The tamer grants his every wish.

On a wet afternoon

This dull and dismal afternoon
Let's go anywhere
Who cares about the rain?
And we run for freedom
All the way to a far off ice-cream kingdom.
In the street we leap
Ice-cream melts, runs like rain
And we wave our palm leaves like
Jesus was here all over again,
And we dance in the streets for him.

We taste the raindrops on the tongue
And we run
Mad with wet fever we plunge
Saturated already
Deeper, deeper out to sea.

No towels, no change of clothes
We slip and squelch on home
We dance in the bathroom
Submerge ourselves in warm calm.

Tears of joy and madness creep
As we sleep
And raindrops explode on empty streets.

Dragon

A dragon walked into a restaurant
His nostrils steaming fiery breath.
"That's a find snout you have there,"
Said the owner rather scared of death
And wanting to make a friend of the dragon
Fearing the dragon might eat him.
"Smoking or non-smoking?"
"You must be joking,"
Replied the dragon, teeth flashing,
Mouth wide open.
"Smoking it is then" and
He led the dragon
To a table for ten
Hoping the dragon could fit in.

The dragon demanded twenty litres of water
And sat there smoking impatiently
Waiting for them to take his order.
"Hmph," he said to himself,
His hot breath singeing the table cloth.
Eventually the waiter arrived:
 "Would you like me to tell you
About the vegetarian special?"
"I want meat and you're very
Lucky I'm not eating people!
Now quick, show me the menu
Otherwise, because I'm a hungry dragon
I might just eat you!"
The dragon snatched the menu
Cast his hungry eyes across it
And sighing, set fire in a fiery fit.

"Rubbish, bring me something big!
I'll have the largest steak in the house, quick!
In fact, bring me the whole cow
And no more waiting, I want it now."
And his angry breath was a hot cloud.
"Right away sir," said the nervous waiter,
"How would you like it cooked,
Well done, medium or rare?"
"I shall flame it myself
At the table right here."
Several firewater whiskies later
They delivered the beast to the dragon's table.
The head waiter looked a little unsure
This had never been done before
And the other guests were silent
Waiting to observe the wonder.
"Stand well back," barked the dragon,
"I shall need a fair bit of room."
The owner politely enquired,
"Was this safe?"
"Of course," dismissed the dragon
Taking a deep breath.
Then came forth the fire jet
And the cow was duly cooked
The owner breathed a sigh of relief
The dragon began his food.

But something stuck in his dragon throat
And a coughing fit ensued
With each little splutter
The dragon's breath grew hotter
And a fiery sea spread further,
The dragon drank more water.

The steam it was too strong
The tongues of fire stretched long.
The restaurant deserted
Guests afraid of being burn-ed.
Someone summoned the Fire Brigade
To quench the mass of yellow flame
And the building it could not be saved
But the staff and dragon did escape.

This short story explains why
By and by
You will never find a dragon
Dining in your local tavern.
They are a danger to the
Public and themselves
And belong in dark places
Along with the wolves
Setting fire to forests, blackening the air
Barbecuing strangers who, foolish, stray round there.

Johnny Wharton

Picked snot
And showed you the lot
In a green and black hand
And just as he planned
You're shocked you yuk
But you can't resist another look.
Johnny belched good
And after milk the letters would
Echo forth from his tunnel throat
And to see our disgust made Johnny gloat.
And to promise a show much more perverse
He would start at the 'Z' and burp in reverse.
He spat
You knew that
But you really didn't mind
'Cos Johnny was harmless and one of a kind.
And you knew in the future all that he'd done
Could be recalled in poems just like this one.

He won't hurt you

I'm still running
He's still coming
-He won't hurt you
-He won't hurt you
His mad eyes glaring
Hear her yelling
-He won't hurt you
-He won't hurt you.
Sharp snout steaming
White teeth gleaming
Strong limbs hurling
Snarl lips curling
-Look at 'im playing
-He's only playing.
Ferocious bark
His claws are sharp
Killer dog flies through the air
Topples me I'm lying there
-He won't hurt you
-He's only playing.
There's the crack of bone
The grind of gristle
My leg is off
I hear her whistle
-He wouldn't hurt you
-He's only playing.
I crawl away
A bloody mess
Injured bad
One leg less.

-I'm sorry luv'
-About your limb
-It's just like him
-Sometimes gets a little excited
-Bites you where you shouldn't be bited
-But he's only playing
-He wouldn't really hurt you
-No, he wouldn't hurt you
-He was only playing, only playing
She says to the tune of ambulance wailing
And here they come with stretcher bearing.
Ferocious dog looks at me sneering
Laughs at what his mistress is saying
-No, I wouldn't hurt you I was only playing
Only, only, only playing

Fishes

In the beginning
There was water, there was land
And the creatures got together
Just as God had planned.
Two fishes met
In a shallow rock pool
One said to
The other, "I do like you."
She waved her tail
And clapped her fins
Then blew some bubbles
Through her shaking gills.
She floated on her tummy
And then upon her back
Lay upon her one side
And then the other flank.
Her scales they did sparkle
Like diamonds in sunlight
She was a swimming jewel
She was a wondrous sight.
Mr. Fish could not resist
"Wow you're such a mover.
Let's get married straight away.
I love you, and no other."
Mrs. Fish did giggle
She coloured brilliant red
"Oh Mr. Fish you're such a dish,"
She went ahead and said.
The next day came the wedding
She in bridal gown
He in top hat, fishy tails
The mermaids gathered round.

And duly gave their blessing
And hoped the fish would be
Happy fish forever together
In fishy harmony.
The honeymoon went swimmingly
It was time to settle down
And Mr. Fish began his plans
For the Fishy family house.
"We'll have water in the bedrooms
And in the rooms below.
Water in the bathroom
And in the toilet too.
We'll have lots of babies
Thousands there will be
So we'll need lots of water
For our huge family."
"Yes," said Mrs. Fish,
"We're such a handsome couple
I'd love a lot of little fish
So cute and blowing bubbles.
So I think we're settled
A shoal of fish we'll be
And fill the water long and wide
As far as you can see.
We can do as we will please
We'll call our home the mighty seas
Millions of us there will be
As far and wide as you can see."

So God he made the land
Then called the rest the seas.
A spacious, salty, floating home
For fishy families.

Boyz n'the bak

The teacher says we all
Ought to listen and
Learn something from this morning.
The teacher is not looking
And the boys are up to something.
Serious looks on attentive faces
They're sneaking towards their usual places.
"We've a visitor this morning, children.
I don't want any embarrassing incident."
And the children nod, "we are innocent."

In the front they're so
Terribly well behaved
Listening to all the
Clever things said.
In the middle the
Faintest sense of unrest,
But goodly children are
Doing their best.

But in the back row
There is continuous
Twittering, giggling,
Nudging, grinning,
Elbow digging.
Otherwise they paint a sign upon their faces
'Boredom – excitement do not come near us'.
Not one will crack they scowl and pout
A sign upon their faces says 'keep out'.

The boys at the back
Think that they're winning
That no-one is watching.
But teacher has an eye on you,
Radar senses all they do.
Teacher's seen it all before
Boys you ought to know the score.

OK boys, we have you surrounded
Put your hands up high
Put your grin and giggle down
And no-one will get hurt.
Move silently to the front of the class
And sit down on you bottom
Without disturbing anyone.
Remember – one false move and
It's outside the headmaster's room!

The boys at the back
They ought to know better.
The boys at the back
They're all back together
At the front.

Hope

A black man on a golf course
Waved his three iron at me
And grinned the widest whitest mouth
The world has ever seen.

Now sir I am not racist
But I like that face it was the kindest of faces
Contrastingly it reminded me of just how mean
And ugly the faces of white people I see
On golf courses self important posh and
Snarling at my kids and me
Proclaiming this you scoundrel is private property.
Now be gone or I shall order the police to come
They are cold and this land is their own
But the black man on the golf course
With the soul and the spirit
Says "Welcome to the promised land
You want to share in it?"
I'm not racist but on golf courses the only friendly faces
Waving three irons like God's golfing angels
Belong to black men who float above the fairways.

Rory goes the wrong way

While we stood and loitered
On solid ground
You danced like a madman
In puddles profound.
With the sun at our backs
We turn to the north
Whilst you turn for sunset
On westerly course.
I was careful descending
To green valley floor
And caught you ascending
To top of brown moor.
Aghast at your lack of cooperation
I threw down the gauntlet
One last proclamation
We're going now, we shall leave you alone!
We're going now, we are heading for home!
We're going now, you'll starve to death!
Die of exposure up here on the heath.
But no answer you did give
Just a shake of the head and a curl of the lips.
"'Tis no matter to me," you say
"For I am Rory – I go the wrong way."

Brothers and sisters

We do, we have to argue
Over size and slice and shape
Of a blob of vanilla ice cream
Or a piece of our favourite cake.
How many hundreds and thousands
Do you have upon that icing?
And what exactly is the radius
Of the sugary doughnut you're eating?
How thick your chocolate topping?
How deep your chocolate mousse?
Don't you dare take one drop more
When sharing out the juice!
Here I'll take the ruler
I think you'll find it's bigger
Here you have the other one
I think you'll find it's smaller
I think you'll find it's you who cheats
You know it yes you do.
Me who cheats? Well that's a laugh!
I think you'll find it's you.
You always have the biggest
I do not! Oh yes you do.
The fingers they are pointing,
There's waving fisties too
You're always telling terrible lies
I do not! Oh yes you do.
Kicking and some screaming,
Now there's crying too.
You it is who always starts
I do not! Oh yes you do.

Bruising and a battering
Now there's trouble too
You it is who's breaking bones
I do not! Oh yes you do!

Brothers and sisters
Were made to tell tales
All about who had done what.
Who had bitten and scratched and pinched
When they ought really have not.

She it was who kicked me
Who dug me with her nails
And all she does is sit there
And scowl at me and wail.
Him who kicked me really hard
Just look at this mark here!
She's sniffing and a-snuffling
She's drowning in her tears.
Him he's just a bully
He always picks on me,
His little princess sister –
Defenceless so petite.

He it is who, open-mouthed
Is sent up to his room
And told he must apologise
Before he can return.
On his bed he contemplates
Just what did I do?
I think it wasn't all me
I think that some was you.

But brothers they were made
To always take the blame
Set up by sneaky sisters
Much sneakier than them.

Clapham Junction

Clapham Junction
How can it function?
All that distraction
Coming and going.
All that compact
Crissing and crossing
Snaking rails
Twisting and turning.
Creeping and crawling
Loud announcements
Clapham is calling.
(Indecision
An engine stalling)
Chaos abounds
The roof is falling.
A major malfunction
At Clapham Junction.

Isn't life funny?

When life is all too miserable
And I mean really unbearable
I should take myself
And jump off a cliff
Or hold my breath under water.
Yes I ought to.
Or simply say
Hey look! I am dead
And then close my eyes
And never speak again.
- But I don't like pain
And I'd like to wake up
And start again.
I'd have myself
Beheaded imperiously
But life's a joke
Honestly, seriously.

Waterloo

Waterloo where people are not on the move
Are immediately clamped between both feet
Where the cost of relieving yourself
Is a staggering twenty pee.
The man behind the counter wears a
Smile as sour as your black coffee.
Pecking pigeons starving, busy
Dive bomb mercilessly.
Our life is little lost fishes
Swimming in a terminal sea
And Waterloo's relaxed trains sit on
Solid rails waiting patiently.

Go to da clinic (e-motion)

I gotta trouble – da police
The law
I say stick it.
The teachers the same
I say they're all
In it.
But my mother and father they say you better change it
That face of you monster you'd better re-arrange it.

You go to da clinic
Put e-motion back in it
You go to da clinic
It's indifference that's in it
You go to da clinic
Put a smile back in it
You go to da clinic
Your face we rebuild it.

I got trouble with me nature
I was
Born with it.
And everything is negative no respect in it
Look at you like I want you to die – in'it
Everyone that's walking by – in'it
I don't even want to try – in'it
So my parents they say man get off to da clinic!

You go to da clinic…

I drive with me friends – we're speeding through it
I smoke with me friends – everyone do it
I run with me friends from the scene of the crime
Some gun may be killed and maybe next time?
I see me TV I see all the papers
No-one smiling no good news for us
Fighting and the-soapy-snore-us
Send us to sleep and deathly bore us!

You go to da clinic...

Hey! Stepped in da clinic got a fairy tale
Some people they was laughing
Someone gave me a smile
There wasn't any hate
There wasn't any vi-ol-ence
In the streets they're going to teach me to dance
Da clinic it's going to give peace a chance
Everyone going to take a new stance
Estonia, Latvia, Spain and France
The President dressed in his President's pants
Hey man we got a global romance!

You go to da clinic...

Bedtime blues

Chorus:
I got the bedtime blues
It swear that it's not late
I got the bedtime blues
Don't send me to my fate
I got the bedtime blues
Don't want to hit the sack
If you send me up those stairs
You know I'll be right back!

It starts about tea time
The rule it has been red
You've had a busy day my boy
It's time for early bed
But I am full of energy
I just want to run around
My brain is working overtime
It won't let me calm down.

Chorus

Come on have a bath dear
You can relax, she said
But this here bath is trickery
The next stop is the bed.
I don't want to soak in bubbles
And splash around in wet
'Cos the next thing that I know
I'll be floating in my bed.

Chorus

Well you say it's getting late
And since I've had my tea
I ought to be a-sleepin'
A little boy like me.
But take a look at my eyes
They're still wide open see
I don't need any matchsticks
A little boy like me.

Chorus

Well you say it's getting later
Time is moving on
But you know that you can't do it
You don't want to steal my fun
I look at you with doey eyes
I shake my little head
Oh Mum have mercy on me!
Don't send me to my bed.

Chorus

Now you say that it is very late
And Daddy's gone to bed
And if I wouldn't mind
You would like to rest your head
But Mummy dear you know
I like to go to bed past ten
Now you creep up those stairs
And I will follow you to bed!

Chorus

Pedestrians, where are you?

Chorus:
There's no room for these pedestrians no more
There's no room for these pedestrians no more
It's all ten tonne trucks
You're out of luck
You're gonna have to leave here
There's no room for you pedestrians no more

Try to walk
Well that's a joke
If the cars miss you
You'll choke on smoke.

Chorus

The bike's not safe
The bus don't come
Get in your car
Like everyone.

Chorus

Train is derailed
The old tram gone
The car is king!
The queue is long!

Chorus

The pavement's gone
The road is wide
No room to walk
No place to ride.

Nowhere to run
Nowhere to hide
Yes the pedestrian has
Died!

Last chorus:
Gotta have room for us pedestrians this time
Gotta have room for us pedestrians this time
If you want a future
And gridlock doesn't suit yer
Must have room for us pedestrians, oh yeah!
Gotta have room for us pedestrians this time
Gotta have room for us pedestrians this time
If you want a future
And gridlock doesn't suit yer
Must have room for us pedestrians, oh yeah!

Don't run me over

Chorus:
Don't run me over
I'm a famous writer
So many wondrous words
I've left to say.
Don't run me over
I'd be kind of dead, yeah
The people need to
Hear my voice today!

Every now and then
It seems a genius is born
All the angels up in Heaven
They were singin' on that morn
They cried "well hallelujah
A saviour is he"
I was born to save the world
You know I mean that literally!

Chorus

Some children they just love to play
Well that is fair enough
But me I couldn't wait
To get working on all that stuff
At six months I was talking
At age one I could write
At eight I'm reading Tolstoy
Got Shakespeare in my sights.

Chorus

Now other kids went dancin'
And had a lot of fun
But me I like to stay at home
A-sharpening my pen.
I learnt to speak in Latin
I thought in ancient Greek
I took my dictionary to bed
To help me off to sleep.

Chorus

Now I didn't have much money
I was penniless and poor
Till I had a story published
They said hey we want some more!
Hey guys this guy is gold dust
I was the biggest hit
Now I'm selling millions
And I'm living like a king.

Chorus

And now I'm writing poetry
And novels by the score
Film scripts, plays and TV sets
And sure there's much much more.
When God was handing gifts out
He gave the pen to me
And when I get to Heaven
I'll write his biography.

Chorus